The Ward Brothers are two brothers who create designs that interest them and make them laugh. Their work is printed on greeting cards, which they sell in UK shops, on their market stall in London and online at Quitegoodcards. com. *Odd Trumps* is their first book.

Thanks to Muz, Gruz, Dmunger
and all our customers and friends
on Broadway Market for your help.

The Ward Brothers

ODD TRUMPS

Pop Culture Gone Weird

BOXTREE

First published 2016 by Boxtree
an imprint of Pan Macmillan
20 New Wharf Road, London N1 9RR
Associated companies throughout the world
www.panmacmillan.com

ISBN 978-0-7522-6618-3

9 8 7 6 5 4 3 2 1

A CIP catalogue record for this book is available from the British Library.

Printed and bound by CPI Group (UK) Ltd, Croydon, CR0 4YY

Visit **www.panmacmillan.com** to read more about all our books
and to buy them. You will also find features, author interviews and
news of any author events, and you can sign up for e-newsletters
so that you're always first to hear about our new releases.

The first Odd Trump we ever did was Adele Boy and it quickly became the most popular card on our market stall. People bought them faster than we could print them. Clearly celebrities and surreal puns go together, we thought. So we did Huge Jackman and Channing Tantrum and that might have been the end of it. But, being brothers, it wasn't enough to create these celebrity mutations, we had to know who would win in a fight.

And once we started, we couldn't stop. Would Miley Virus clobber Beeyoncé? Does Judi Hench have too much for Kanye Pest? Is Britney's spear or Jeremy's iron the better weapon?

This book is an attempt to lay these important questions to rest so we can all get on with our lives.

We'll see you on the battlefield.

The Ward Brothers

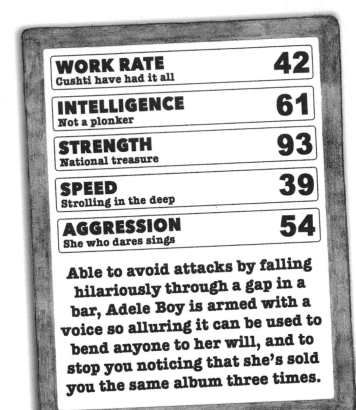

WORK RATE Cushti have had it all	**42**
INTELLIGENCE Not a plonker	**61**
STRENGTH National treasure	**93**
SPEED Strolling in the deep	**39**
AGGRESSION She who dares sings	**54**

Able to avoid attacks by falling hilariously through a gap in a bar, Adele Boy is armed with a voice so alluring it can be used to bend anyone to her will, and to stop you noticing that she's sold you the same album three times.

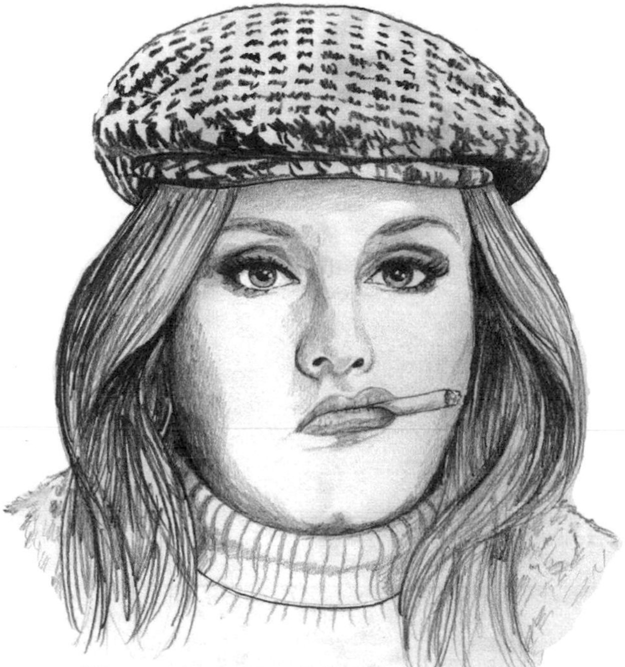

ADELE BOY

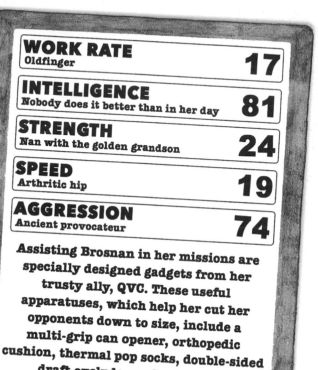

WORK RATE
Oldfinger
17

INTELLIGENCE
Nobody does it better than in her day
81

STRENGTH
Nan with the golden grandson
24

SPEED
Arthritic hip
19

AGGRESSION
Ancient provocateur
74

Assisting Brosnan in her missions are specially designed gadgets from her trusty ally, QVC. These useful apparatuses, which help her cut her opponents down to size, include a multi-grip can opener, orthopedic cushion, thermal pop socks, double-sided draft excluder and, of course, the invisible mobility scooter.

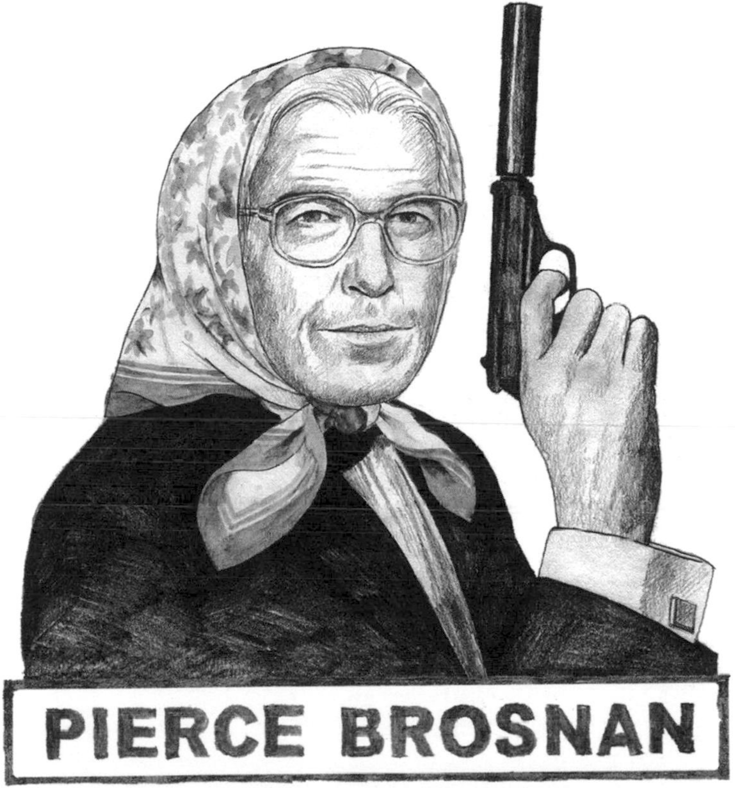
PIERCE BROSNAN

WORK RATE 9 to 5	95
INTELLIGENCE Country bumpkin	27
STRENGTH Granny winner	30
SPEED Nip 'n' tuck	61
AGGRESSION She means business	74

Famous for her discipline and physical bravery, it is said that Dolly Spartan was able to keep an entire army at bay using only her folksy home-spun wisdom, catchy melodies and enormous rhinestone bra.

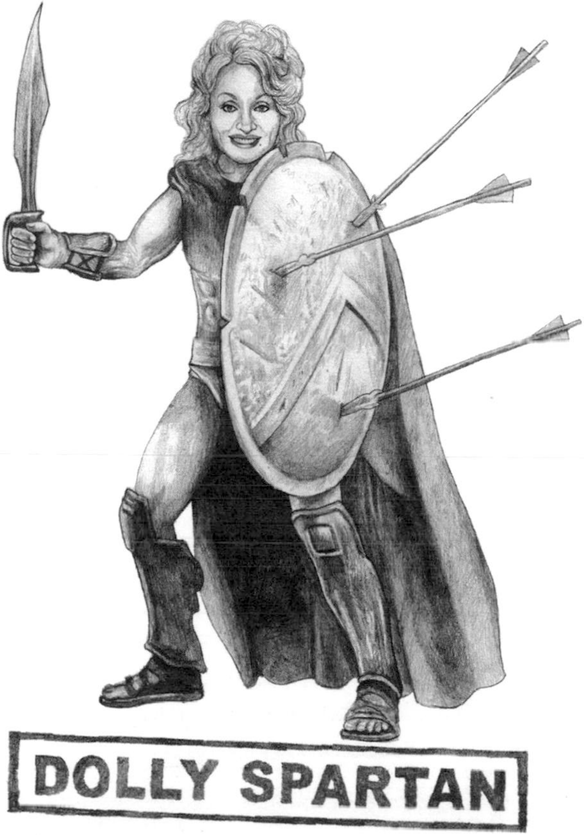

DOLLY SPARTAN

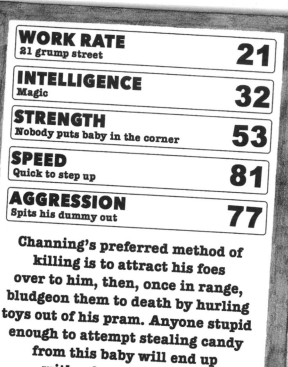

WORK RATE
21 grump street
21

INTELLIGENCE
Magic
32

STRENGTH
Nobody puts baby in the corner
53

SPEED
Quick to step up
81

AGGRESSION
Spits his dummy out
77

Channing's preferred method of killing is to attract his foes over to him, then, once in range, bludgeon them to death by hurling toys out of his pram. Anyone stupid enough to attempt stealing candy from this baby will end up with a face full of pain.

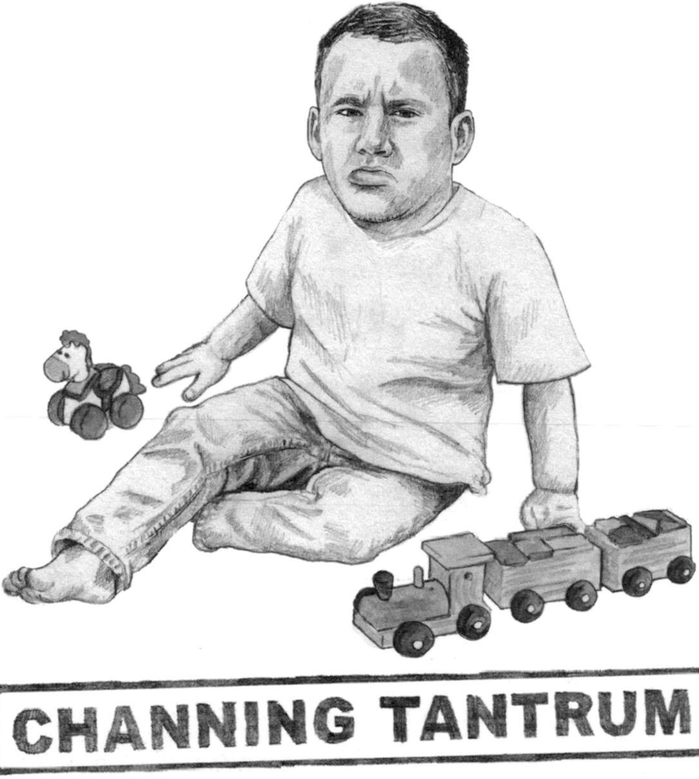

CHANNING TANTRUM

WORK RATE
He's very hard work

87

INTELLIGENCE
IQ is one of the highest

11

STRENGTH
Hair-raising

80

SPEED
Slow moving but relentless

03

AGGRESSION
You're fired

90

If given half a chance The Donald will envelop his prey in his oily folds and suffocate them under the weight of his self-importance, leaving their putrefied carcasses in his wake. The only defence is to build a wall to keep him out, or, failing that, just pour salt over his body.

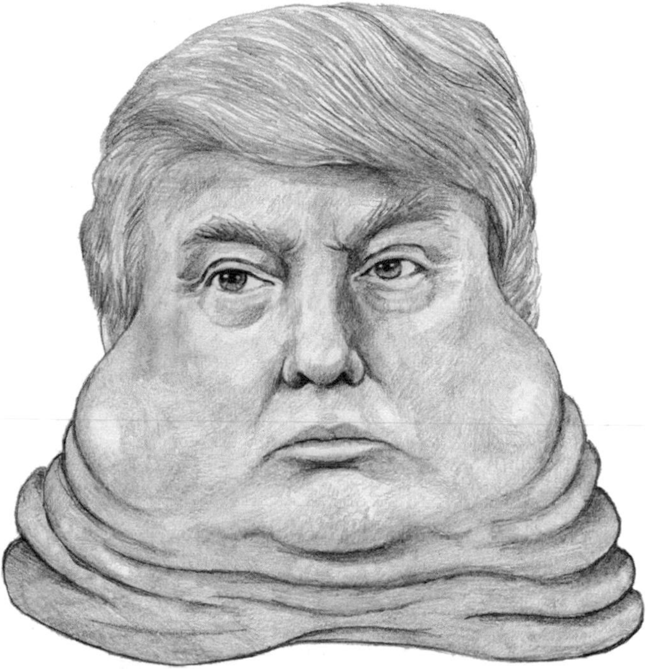

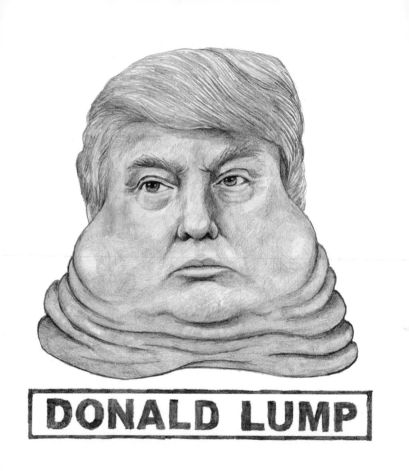

DONALD LUMP

WORK RATE Stressed. Look at the furrowed brow	**84**
INTELLIGENCE A genius compared to the other guy...	**52**
STRENGTH Luckily can afford health care	**49**
SPEED Quicker than Lewinsky's dry-cleaner	**69**
AGGRESSION We got him	**78**

Born of a bellicose people rooted in war, violence and weaponry – or Americans, as you might know them – Hillary is aiming to become the first woman to lead the clan. She might struggle, as her manifesto is full of limp-wristed liberal pledges like free cuddles, the compulsory wearing of trouser suits and background checks on assault weapons.

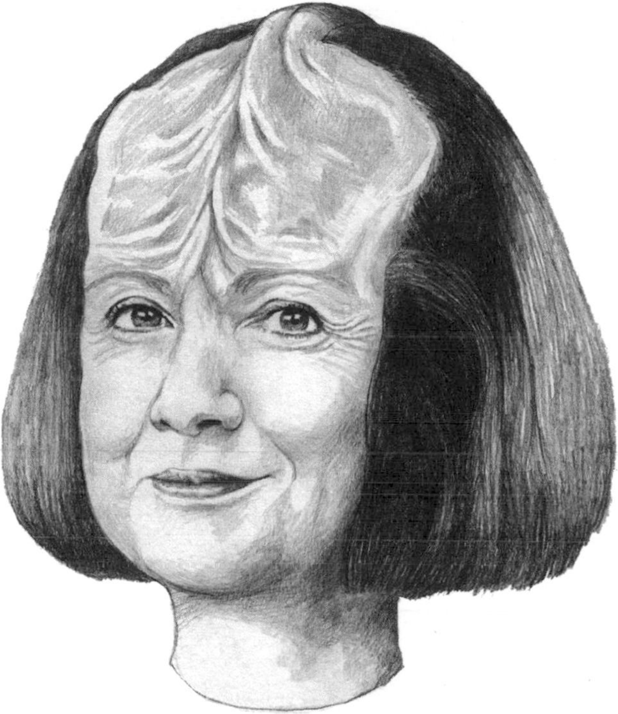

HILLARY KLINGON

WORK RATE 22
Not a hard work life

INTELLIGENCE 76
Empire state of mind

STRENGTH 80
Big pimpin'

SPEED 46
Run this town tonight

AGGRESSION 20
Lazy right now

No one is exactly sure how deadly Lay Z is, as they've never been able to get him to turn up to a fight. Instead he sits in his comfy chair listing his 99 problems, which include his phone always running out of battery, and his sandwich being so big it hurts his mouth to eat.

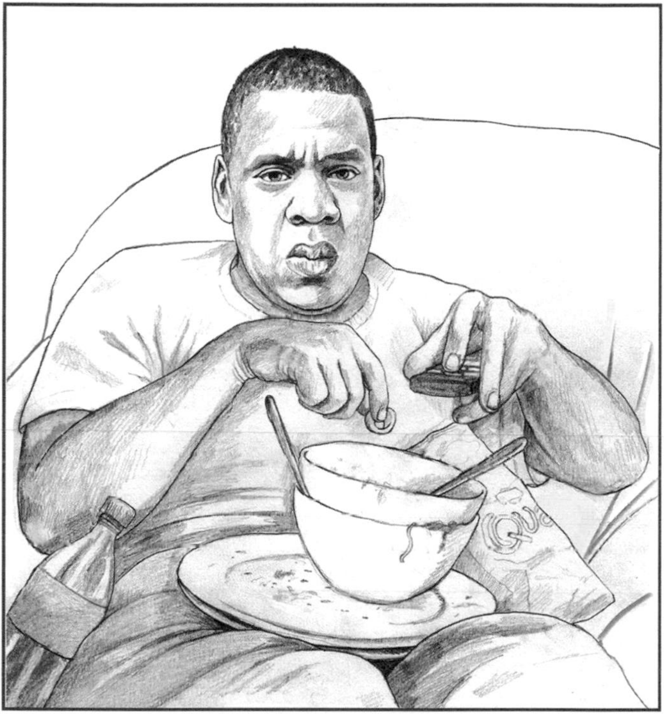

LAY Z

WORK RATE Has drive	**73**
INTELLIGENCE Crazy stupid, love	**33**
STRENGTH Big, short	**50**
SPEED Quicker than a 'Hey girl' meme	**84**
AGGRESSION Wields a Mickey Mouse club	**18**

Behind this adorable creature's fluffy hair and come-to-bed eyes lurks a vicious killer. The Ryan Gosling will draw you in with his cuteness, but when you drop your guard he'll strike. Can often be found by following groups of salivating women.

RYAN GOSLING

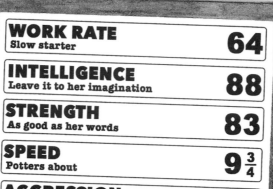

WORK RATE
Slow starter

64

INTELLIGENCE
Leave it to her imagination

88

STRENGTH
As good as her words

83

SPEED
Potters about

9¾

AGGRESSION
Stay in her good books

48

This millionaire author and tacit supporter of witchcraft attacks with a series of teddy-bear rolls until her opponent can no longer tell if they're an adult or a child. They then agree to follower her, no matter what. These deluded followers will even run through brick walls for her, especially in King's Cross station.

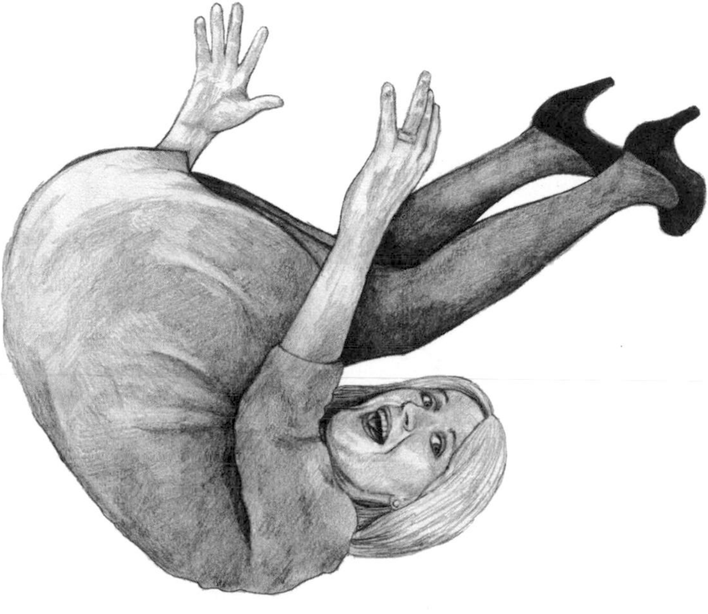

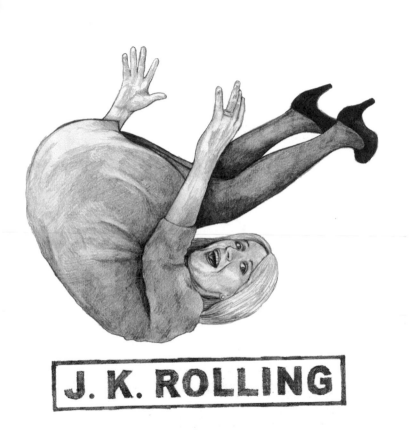

J. K. ROLLING

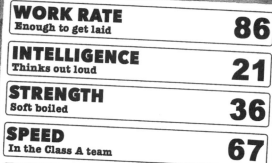

WORK RATE
Enough to get laid
86

INTELLIGENCE
Thinks out loud
21

STRENGTH
Soft boiled
36

SPEED
In the Class A team
67

AGGRESSION
Runs for the eggsit
05

Egg Sheeran has the genial air of a friend who always brings his guitar to a BBQ. In many countries it is now illegal to get married without one of his songs being played as the first dance. It is thought that if the couple can get through the tedious banality of his music, married life will be one long honeymoon.

EGG SHEERAN

WORK RATE
A slave for you **78**

INTELLIGENCE
Not that innocent **55**

STRENGTH
Toxic **84**

SPEED
Quick change **63**

AGGRESSION
In the zone **77**

Before her triumphant return to Vegas, Britney had secretly trained with Shaolin monks to master the sacred art of the Qiang (the spear). A placid character unless repeatedly provoked, the first hit you land will get her attention, but if you dare hit her one more time that'll be the last thing you'll do.

BRITNEY SPEARS

WORK RATE
Work, Work, Work, Work, Work
91

INTELLIGENCE
Room for improvement
37

STRENGTH
Can work his magic
47

SPEED
Slithering
24

AGGRESSION
Smooth
26

Just before he strikes, the Drake O'Malfoy will perform his distinctive attack dance which consists of shuffling slowly from side to side like a toddler who needs a poo. His spells can be powerful, but a weakness for chunky knitwear means he is vulnerable to water.

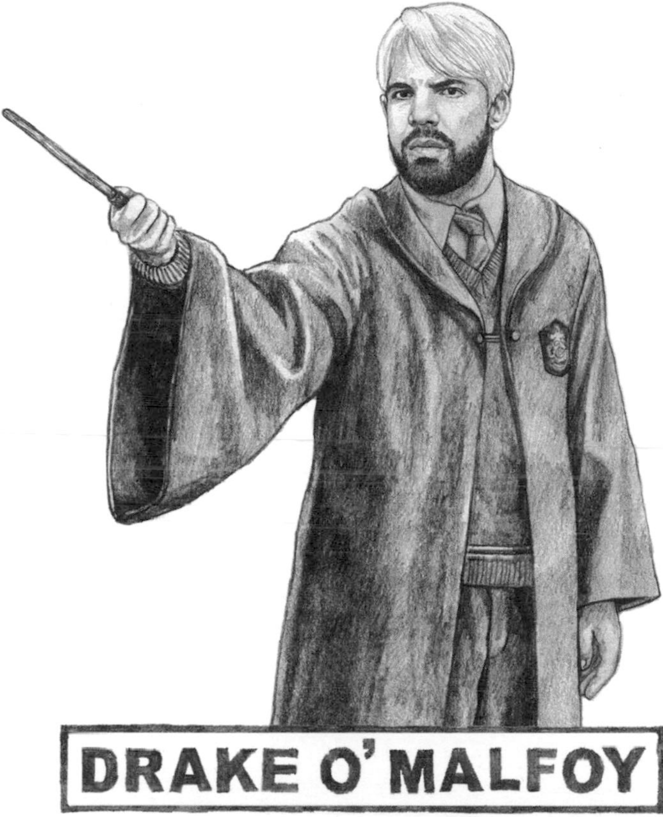

DRAKE O' MALFOY

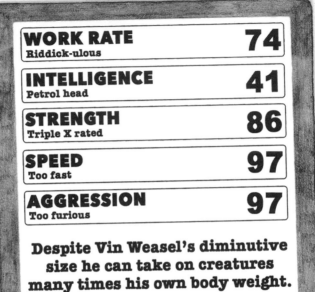

WORK RATE Riddick-ulous	**74**
INTELLIGENCE Petrol head	**41**
STRENGTH Triple X rated	**86**
SPEED Too fast	**97**
AGGRESSION Too furious	**97**

Despite **Vin Weasel's** diminutive size he can take on creatures many times his own body weight. Once he gets started there's no stopping him and with 'The Fast and the Furriest 68: Milton Keynes Meltdown' due out this year, it may never end.

VIN WEASEL

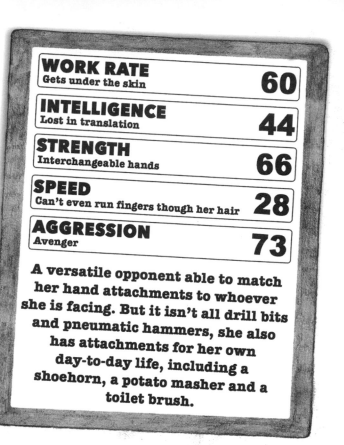

WORK RATE
Gets under the skin
60

INTELLIGENCE
Lost in translation
44

STRENGTH
Interchangeable hands
66

SPEED
Can't even run fingers though her hair
28

AGGRESSION
Avenger
73

A versatile opponent able to match her hand attachments to whoever she is facing. But it isn't all drill bits and pneumatic hammers, she also has attachments for her own day-to-day life, including a shoehorn, a potato masher and a toilet brush.

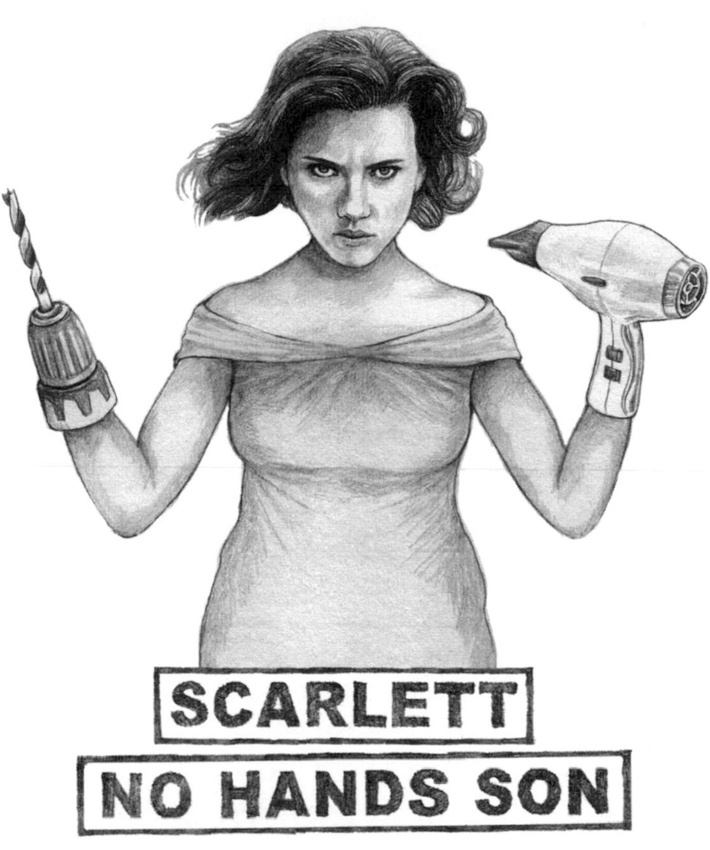
SCARLETT
NO HANDS SON

WORK RATE	54
All shook up	

INTELLIGENCE	62
Suspicious mind	

STRENGTH	77
Light footed	

SPEED	56
Now or never	

AGGRESSION	65
Nothing but a pound dog	

During combat, Elfish will curl his lip, bearing his teeth before he strikes, and his nimble footwork makes him virtually unbeatable. It's no wonder his enemies don't want to believe he's coming back, but his followers can't wait for the return of the King.

ELFISH PRESLEY

WORK RATE
Virgin on the ridiculous

98

INTELLIGENCE
Ray of light straight through her ears

04

STRENGTH
Chilli sauce

71

SPEED
Frozen

11

AGGRESSION
Gone vogue

39

Fighting Madonner may seem like a good idea at 1 a.m., but when her opponents wake in the morning they will be full of regret. A relatively slow-moving foe, she makes up for her lack of speed with staying power and a ferociously trained core. All who face her die in agony, kneeling at the toilet as if in prayer.

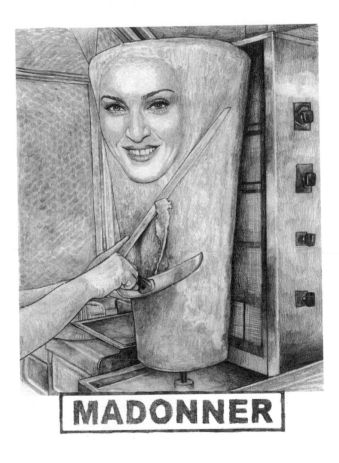

MADONNER

WORK RATE
You see him more than your family
95

INTELLIGENCE
I'm a beleaver
05

STRENGTH
Doesn't give a dam
12

SPEED
Fast in water
91

AGGRESSION
Defending territory from paparazzi
56

Originally only found in Canadian waters, he is now everywhere. Will mate for life with himself and possesses a dangerous bite. If bitten, you will contract 'Beaver Fever'. Symptoms include high-pitched screaming and a hankering for bubble-gum flavoured lip gloss.

JUSTIN BEAVER

WORK RATE
Basically took 1979–1994 off

09

INTELLIGENCE
Tell me more, tell me more!

64

STRENGTH
Stayin' alive

70

SPEED
It's electrifying

88

AGGRESSION
Tear your face/off

95

After bewitching his opponent with hypnotizing dialogue about what the French call fast food, Tra-vaulta strikes. Blessed with densely packed, fast twitch muscles in his thighs, he can summon enough power to propel himself at any would-be assailant.

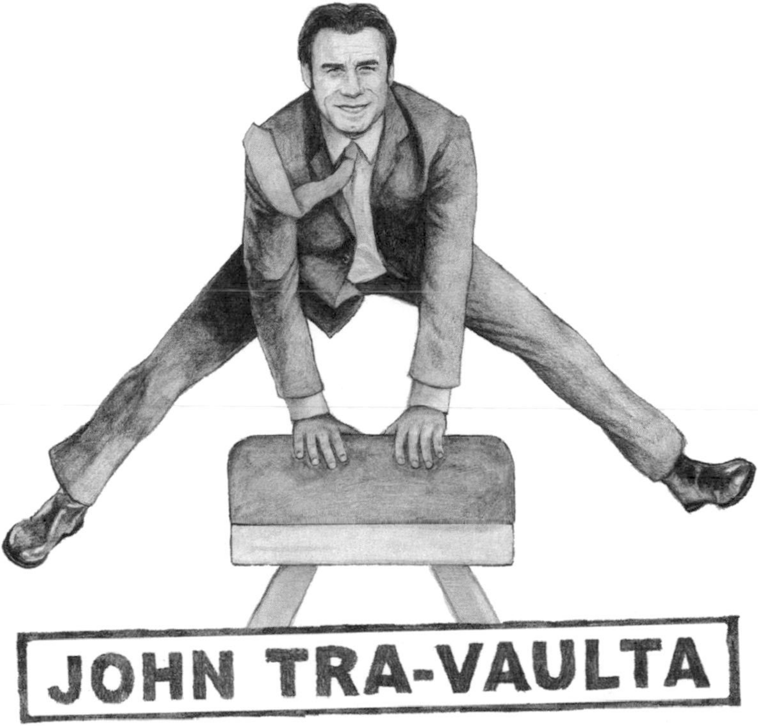

JOHN TRA-VAULTA

WORK RATE	**05**
Wings it	

INTELLIGENCE	**04**
Bird brain	

STRENGTH	**03**
Never misses leg day	

SPEED	**02**
25 mins per 500g	

AGGRESSION	**01**
Can't we all just get along?	

It is normal for prey like Gwyneth to have developed adaptations to prevent being eaten by predators and she is no exception. With no real ability to attack, she has developed a taste so bland, banal and boring that just one little bite will have any predator consciously uncoupling their own head from their body.

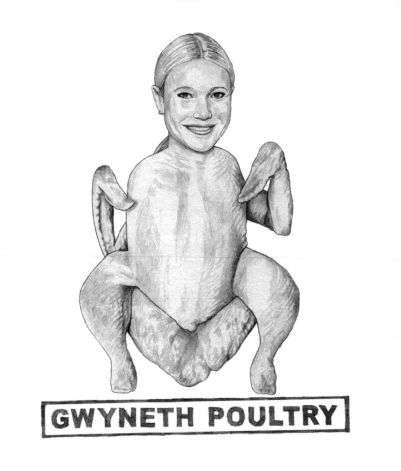

GWYNETH POULTRY

WORK RATE
This train don't stop there anymore — **38**

INTELLIGENCE
Rocket (science) man — **90**

STRENGTH
He's still standing — **32**

SPEED
Tiny advancer — **28**

AGGRESSION
Alright for fighting — **52**

In an effort to lose weight, Meltin' John tried an experimental procedure where wax was injected into his body to replace excess fat. Although initially successful, the unforeseen side-effects were shocking. Able to soften his body at will, he is a cunning foe.

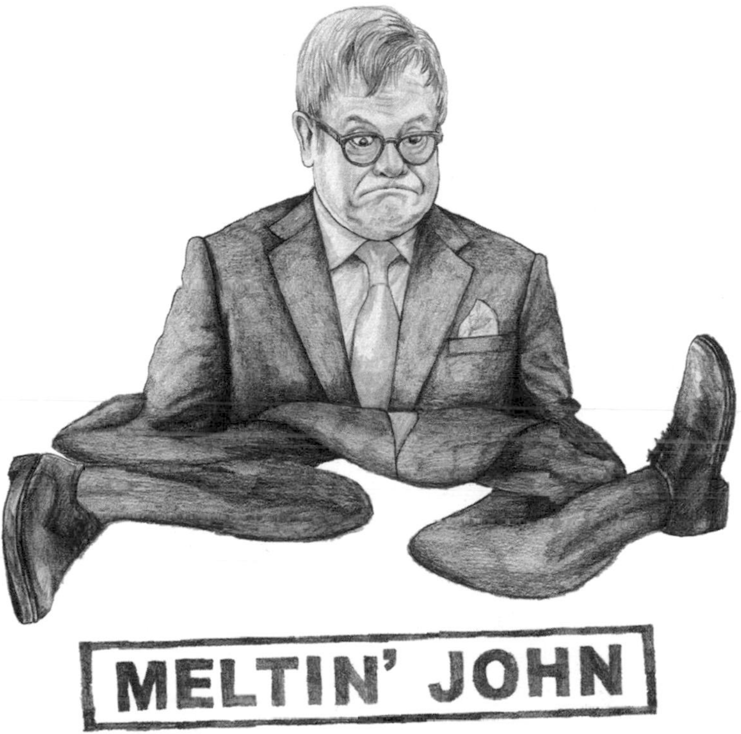

MELTIN' JOHN

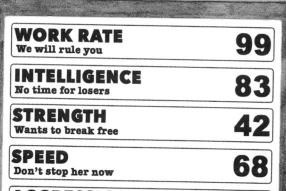

WORK RATE	
We will rule you	**99**

INTELLIGENCE	
No time for losers	**83**

STRENGTH	
Wants to break free	**42**

SPEED	
Don't stop her now	**68**

AGGRESSION	
Ma'am, just killed a man	**77**

An accidental side effect of Brian May playing on top of Buckingham Palace was the creation of Queen, a terrifying blend of inherited privilege and theatrical rock. Queen waits for her opponent to curtsy, then smashes the back of their skull in with her weird little jewel-encrusted mic stick.

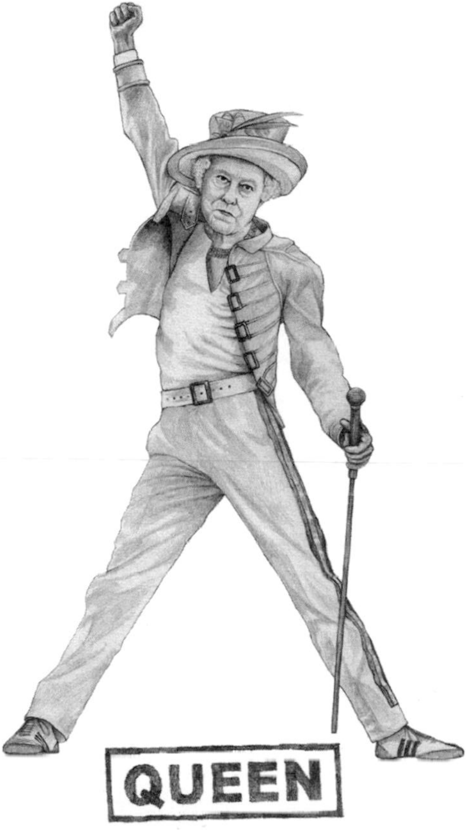
QUEEN

WORK RATE
Forty days and forty nights

40

INTELLIGENCE
Judean psycho

57

STRENGTH
Always carrying people

71

SPEED
Fast, during Lent

24

AGGRESSION
Cross

50

Christian Bale boasts supernatural powers as well as a very short temper. Born in the UK, Christ the Misdemeanor is wanted for a string of offences. These include turning water into Molotov cocktails, and the beating of the 5,000, where he bludgeoned thousands of innocent people with loaves of bread and fish.

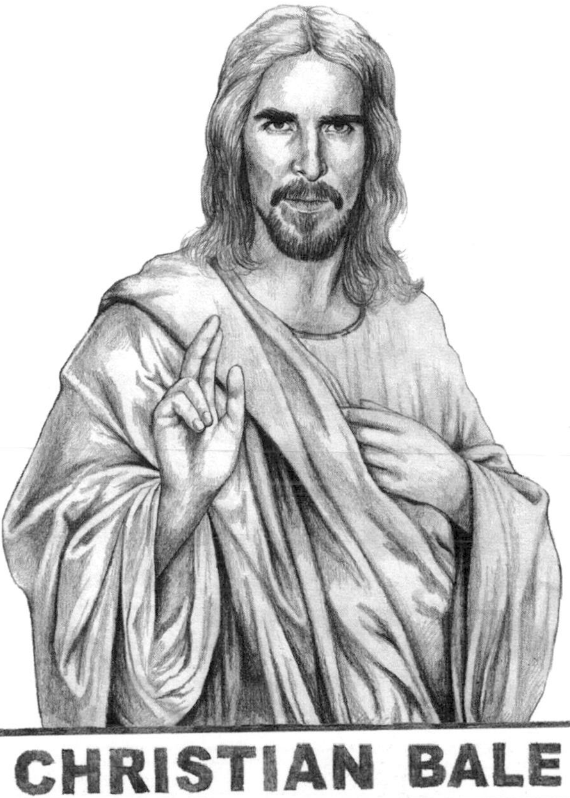

CHRISTIAN BALE

| **WORK RATE** | **01** |
| Only once a year | |

| **INTELLIGENCE** | **14** |
| Muscle memory | |

| **STRENGTH** | **89** |
| Sleighs all before him | |

| **SPEED** | **73** |
| Does quick splits | |

| **AGGRESSION** | **94** |
| High. A rebel with a Coors | |

Santa Claude decides if you should be spared or destroyed based on how good you've been this year. If he finds so much as an unpaid parking ticket, vengeance will be total. You better watch out, you better not cry, you better not pout, I'm telling you why: Santa Claude is coming to batter your face into a bloody pulp.

SANTA CLAUDE

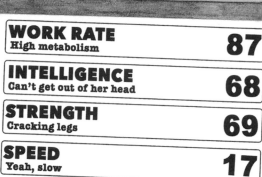

| **WORK RATE** High metabolism | **87** |

| **INTELLIGENCE** Can't get out of her head | **68** |

| **STRENGTH** Cracking legs | **69** |

| **SPEED** Yeah, slow | **17** |

| **AGGRESSION** Neighbour from hell | **60** |

In order to finally get noticed stateside, Kylie developed a serum that when ingested transforms her into a twenty-foot ogre. Unfortunately, as well as being highly addictive, it made her go mad, and the voices in her head won't let her stop taking it. 'Come on baby, do that loco potion,' they continuously whisper.

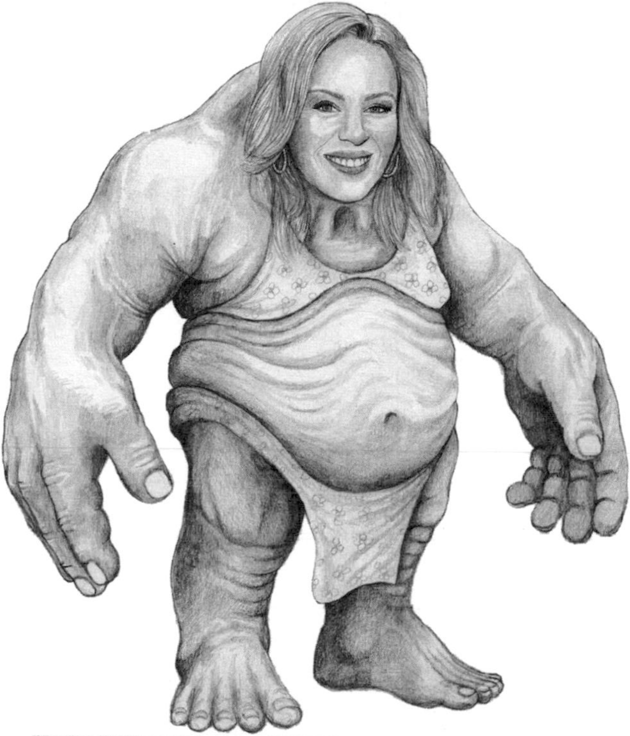

KYLIE MIN-OGRE

| **WORK RATE** | **45** |

He's in literally every X-men film

| **INTELLIGENCE** | **18** |

Head in the clouds

| **STRENGTH** | **77** |

Gets noticed in a crowd

| **SPEED** | **89** |

Always just one step ahead

| **AGGRESSION** | **88** |

Perpetually hangry

The result of nuclear testing in the Pacific Ocean, Huge Jackman can only be lured towards civilization with the promise of yet another Wolverine Origins movie. He causes absolute carnage across the city but, like his performances, once he leaves, all is quickly forgotten and people move on with their lives.

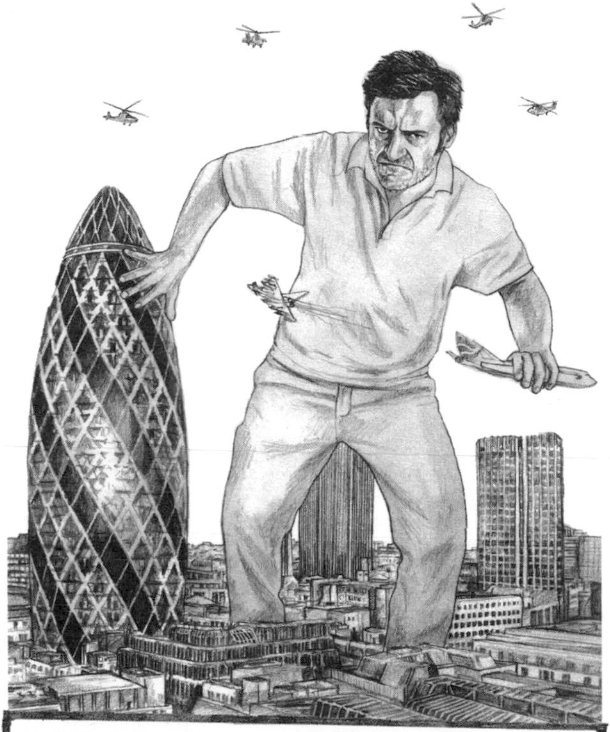

HUGE JACKMAN

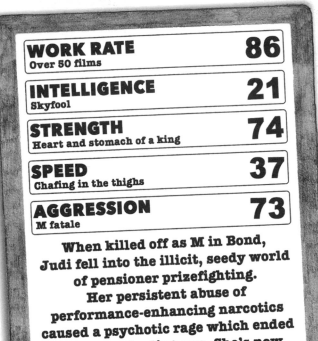

WORK RATE	86
Over 50 films	

INTELLIGENCE	21
Skyfool	

STRENGTH	74
Heart and stomach of a king	

SPEED	37
Chafing in the thighs	

AGGRESSION	73
M fatale	

When killed off as M in Bond,
Judi fell into the illicit, seedy world
of pensioner prizefighting.
Her persistent abuse of
performance-enhancing narcotics
caused a psychotic rage which ended
her career in disgrace. She's now
forced to earn money on the docks
crushing hazelnuts in her biceps
for pervy sailors.

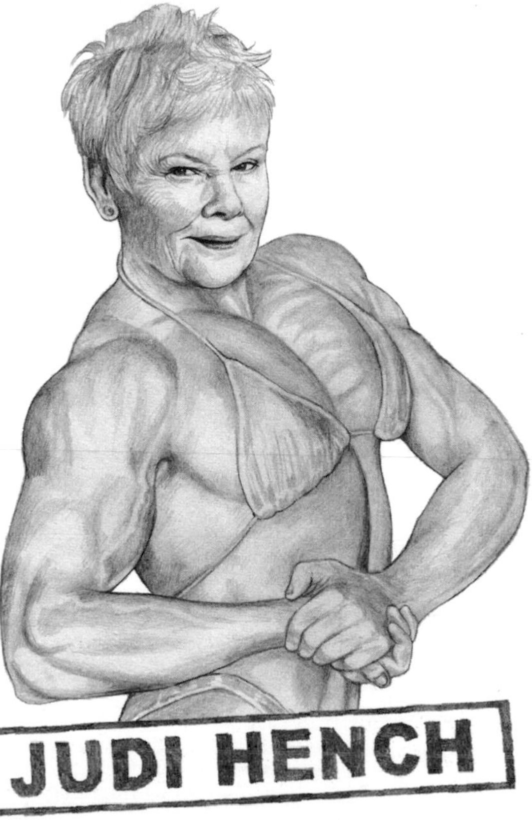

JUDI HENCH

WORK RATE	**80**
Always cooking up something	

INTELLIGENCE	**03**
Rock bottom	

STRENGTH	**88**
Vast and glorious	

SPEED	**94**
Too fast, too fabulous	

AGGRESSION	**58**
No girl's blouse	

Tired of only wearing his pants in the ring and on screen, The Frock decided to get dressy. Armed with a deadly set of killer heels, The Frock finishes off his opponents by trapping them underneath his frilly plumage. You can't smell what The Frock is cooking but you can get an idea of what he had for dinner.

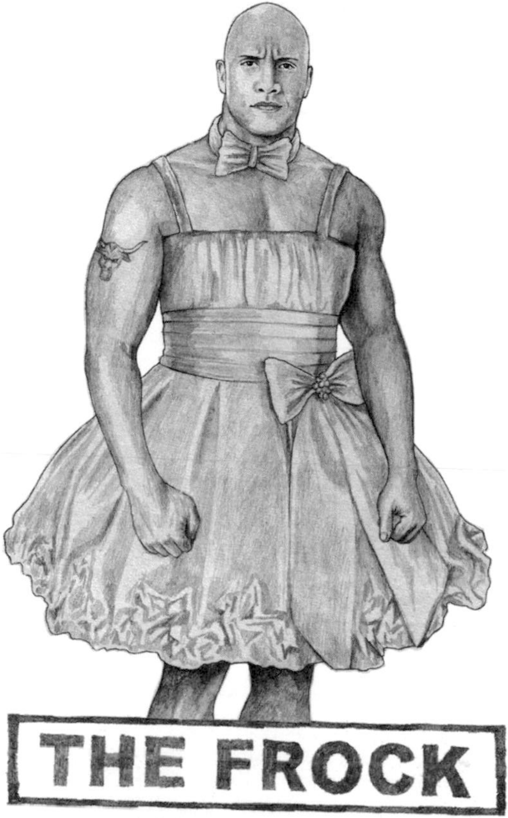
THE FROCK

WORK RATE **55**
Small-screen star

INTELLIGENCE **22**
Lost in face

STRENGTH **64**
Wins friends and influences people

SPEED **37**
Always stuck in second gear

AGGRESSION **70**
He'll be there for you

Matt can perfectly mimic the
appearance of anyone he sets his
eyes on. Unfortunately, he doesn't
have eyes to see any of the facial
features he wants to reproduce. He
is stuck with only being able to
formulate faces created by his
imagination, which, as you can tell,
isn't very useful.

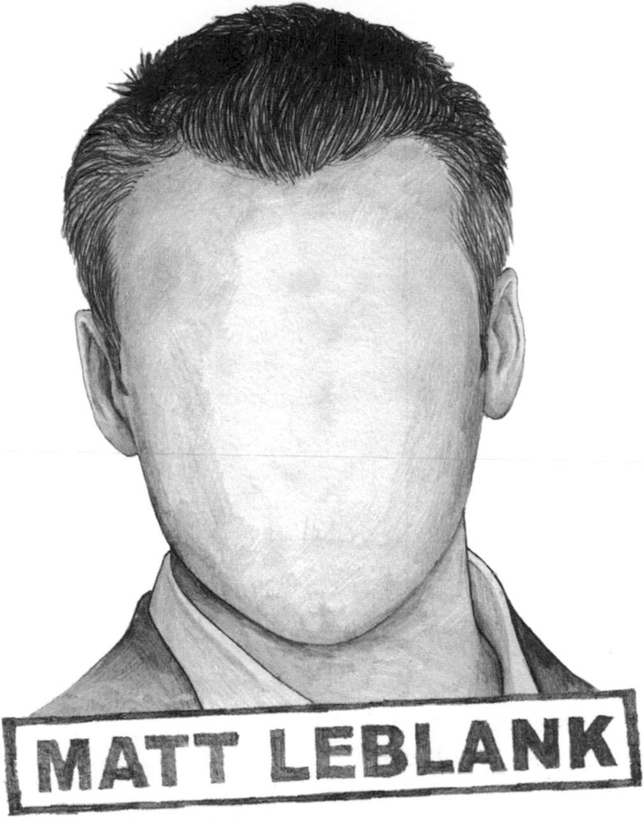
MATT LEBLANK

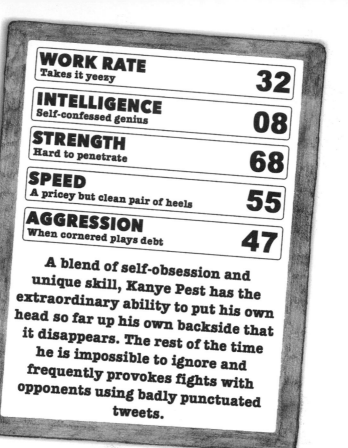

WORK RATE
Takes it yeezy

32

INTELLIGENCE
Self-confessed genius

08

STRENGTH
Hard to penetrate

68

SPEED
A pricey but clean pair of heels

55

AGGRESSION
When cornered plays debt

47

A blend of self-obsession and unique skill, Kanye Pest has the extraordinary ability to put his own head so far up his own backside that it disappears. The rest of the time he is impossible to ignore and frequently provokes fights with opponents using badly punctuated tweets.

KANYE PEST

WORK RATE
Twerk rate excellent

74

INTELLIGENCE
Wiley Cyrus

52

STRENGTH
Like a wrecking ball

88

SPEED
She can't stop

98

AGGRESSION
Can't be tamed

85

Miley is patient zero of a mysterious and dehumanizing virus with terrifying effects. Early symptoms include tolerating Robin Thicke, and prolonged tongue extension. In later stages, this moves to using 'z' in words where there is no 'z' and perpetual nakedness. In 99 per cent of all cases, death comes from an Achy Breaky Heart.

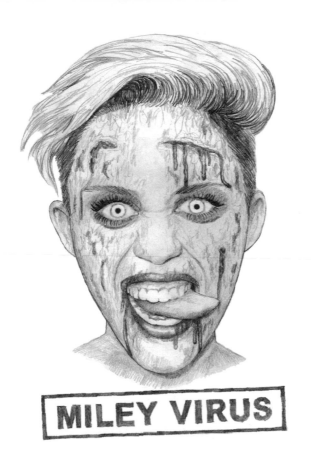

MILEY VIRUS

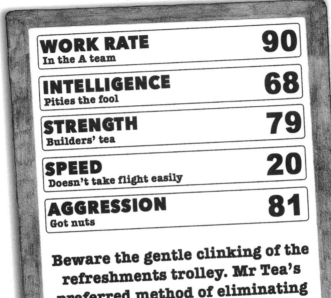

WORK RATE 90
In the A team

INTELLIGENCE 68
Pities the fool

STRENGTH 79
Builders' tea

SPEED 20
Doesn't take flight easily

AGGRESSION 81
Got nuts

Beware the gentle clinking of the refreshments trolley. Mr Tea's preferred method of eliminating his targets is sedative-laced hot drinks followed by choking his victims to death by force-feeding them Garibaldi biscuits.

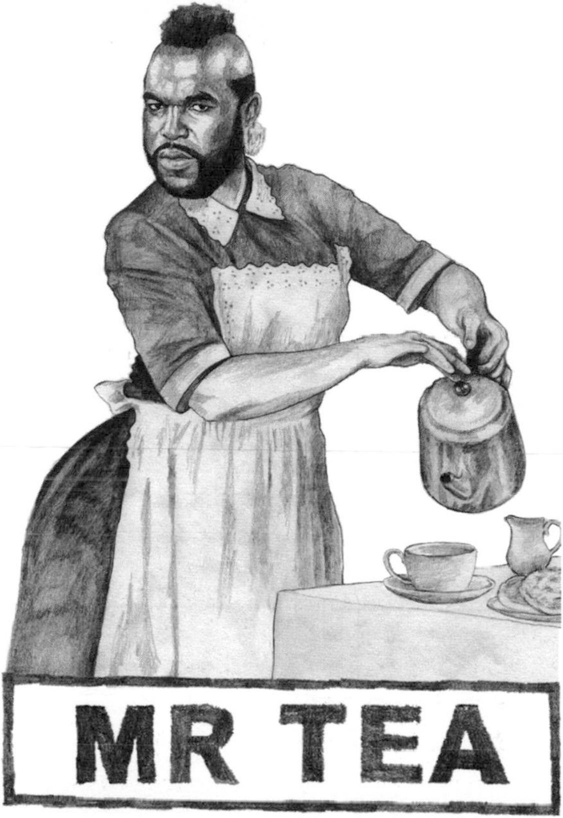
MR TEA

WORK RATE
Maximus doingus thethingeus

83

INTELLIGENCE
A beautiful mind

81

STRENGTH
On his signal, unleash hell

87

SPEED
Superman's dad

94

AGGRESSION
Crow = Duck!

89

The Russell Crow will defend his territory as a 'proper actor' with loud displays in ever-stranger accents. He regurgitates his food to his young using the same technique that he employs to play the same one-dimensional brooding characters in pretty much every film he has ever been in.

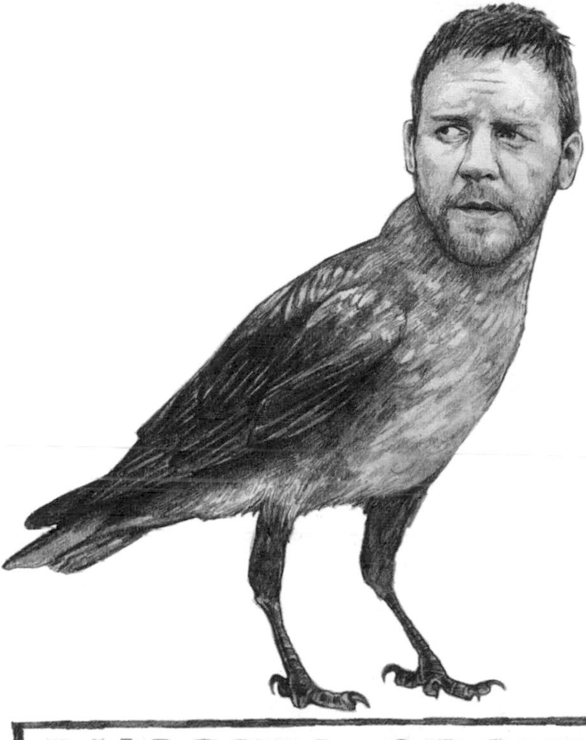

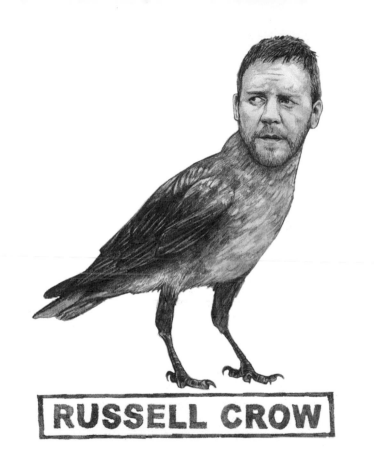

RUSSELL CROW

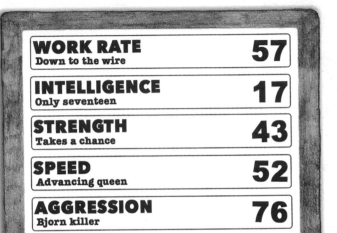

WORK RATE	57
Down to the wire	

INTELLIGENCE	17
Only seventeen	

STRENGTH	43
Takes a chance	

SPEED	52
Advancing queen	

AGGRESSION	76
Bjorn killer	

Idris Abba's life changed when he was attacked by an unknown assailant who threw sequins in his eyes. They lodged in his retina, creating a rare condition called 'Euro Vision'. This debilitating affliction causes the sufferer to believe they are stuck in the last century and to lose all self-awareness. Beware his battle cry 'loofah!'.

IDRIS ABBA

WORK RATE	29
American idle	

INTELLIGENCE	70
Out of sight	

STRENGTH	08
Will get you on the floor	

SPEED	36
Slow out the blocks	

AGGRESSION	27
Looks for resolution	

Incredibly nimble due to her small file size, Jennifer uses her ability to self-pixelate as camouflage to confuse and frustrate opponents. When up-close it's almost impossible to see through her digital disguise. It's only when she's at a distance and making her escape that you can tell its Jenny from the blocks.

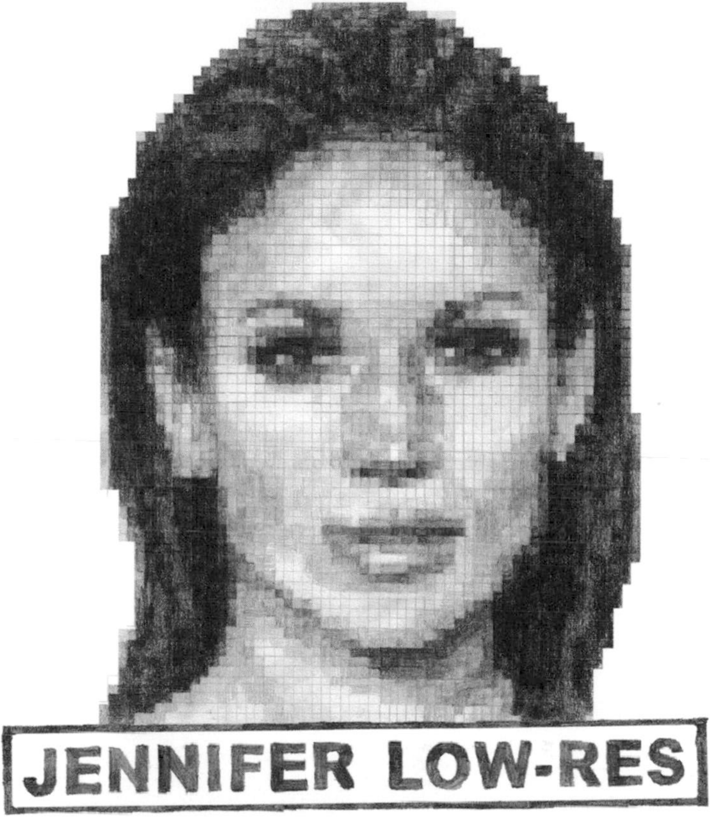
JENNIFER LOW-RES

WORK RATE
Doesn't stop till he gets enough
94

INTELLIGENCE
Django unhinged
76

STRENGTH
Bad
03

SPEED
Quicker backwards than forwards
55

AGGRESSION
Great vengeance and furious anger
87

Armed with rapid foot-speed, devastating choreography and a languid style of delivery, this smooth criminal knows how to beat it with the best of them. By holding his crotch and quickly moving his feet on any carpeted surface, he can pump friction through his body to charge his stylish metallic gauntlet – zapping his prey with electricity.

SAMUEL L. JACKSON

WORK RATE
Slack sparrow

31

INTELLIGENCE
Mad as a hatter

43

STRENGTH
Immersing himself in a role

68

SPEED
Out of his depth

44

AGGRESSION
Makes mountains out of molehills

72

Johnny was approached to play a Soviet double agent in a low budget Nordic arthouse movie. He got the wrong end of the stick and embodied an actual mole. With his mind frazzled and eyesight diminished from years in darkness, Johnny now lives in a vast network of tunnels feasting on earthworms and insect larvae.

JOHNNY DEEP

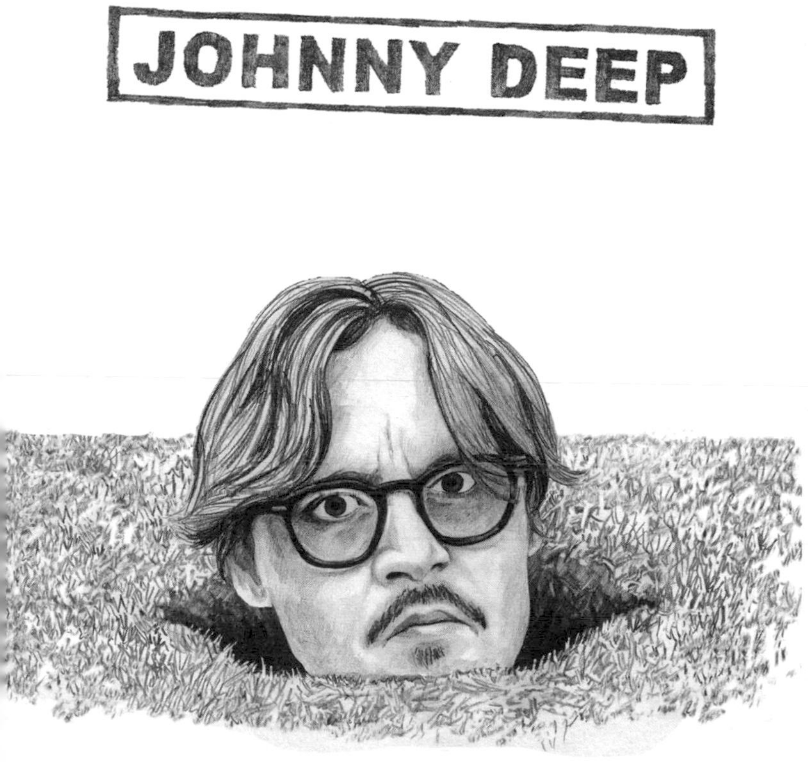

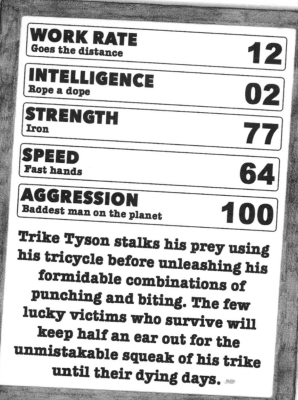

WORK RATE
Goes the distance
12

INTELLIGENCE
Rope a dope
02

STRENGTH
Iron
77

SPEED
Fast hands
64

AGGRESSION
Baddest man on the planet
100

Trike Tyson stalks his prey using his tricycle before unleashing his formidable combinations of punching and biting. The few lucky victims who survive will keep half an ear out for the unmistakable squeak of his trike until their dying days.

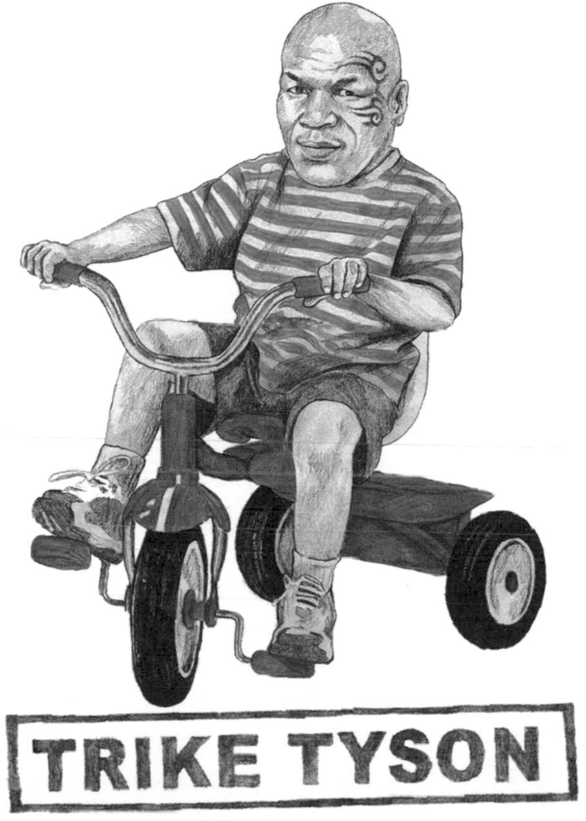

TRIKE TYSON

WORK RATE
Her blood is thicker than water

41

INTELLIGENCE
Fool's gold

10

STRENGTH
Can break the internet

83

SPEED
Try keeping up

86

AGGRESSION
Not too arsey

42

It's hard to know exactly what it is Slim Kardashian actually does. This central question is the essence of her power: you can't destroy nothing. When she is attacked it only adds to her strength and the assailant will become exhausted well before they can make any impact. At which point her sisters appear.

SLIM KARDASHIAN

| WORK RATE | 54 |
| Dry hard | |

| INTELLIGENCE | 61 |
| Daytime TV quiz genius | |

| STRENGTH | 52 |
| The lining king | |

| SPEED | 78 |
| 8 shirts in 15 mins | |

| AGGRESSION | 67 |
| Broadside revisited | |

Armed with a TurboSteam 3000 – with ceramic base plate and a rather long extension cable – Jeremy patrols the streets, melting unsavoury villains using his weapon's blisteringly hot cotton setting. To make his escape he switches to full steam mode and disappears into the mist.

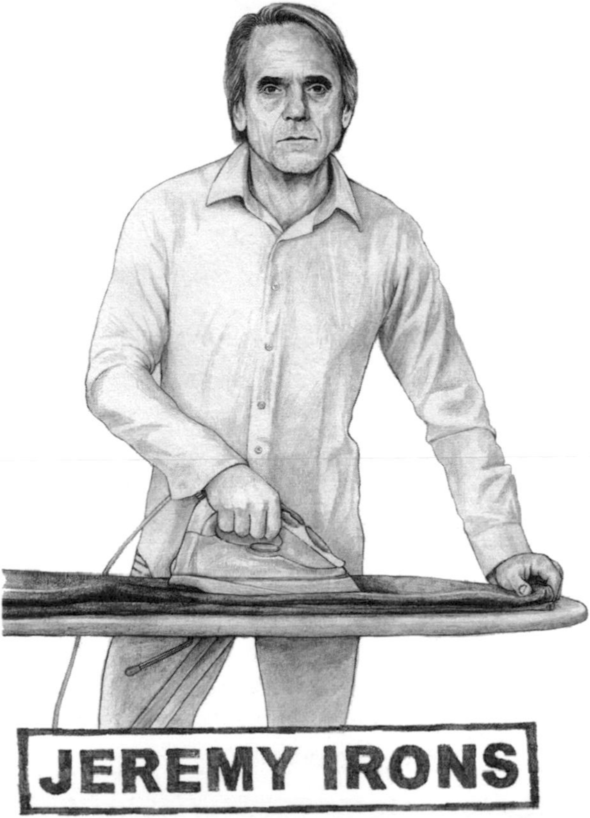
JEREMY IRONS

WORK RATE — Part-time lover — **50**

INTELLIGENCE — Superstitious — **16**

STRENGTH — Will modown his enemies — **72**

SPEED — Signed, sealed, delivered — **88**

AGGRESSION — Takes the higher ground — **40**

Isn't he lovely? Isn't he won-der-ful? Well no, he's not. Using his powerful vocal cords, Stevie can produce dense sound-waves that can tear apart the atoms in his opponents' bodies. Don't try to understand things you can't believe, just get the hell out of his way.

STEVIE WONDER

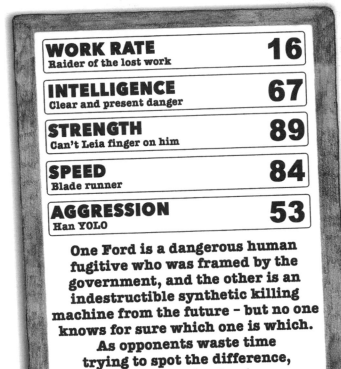

| WORK RATE | **16** |
| Raider of the lost work | |

| INTELLIGENCE | **67** |
| Clear and present danger | |

| STRENGTH | **89** |
| Can't Leia finger on him | |

| SPEED | **84** |
| Blade runner | |

| AGGRESSION | **53** |
| Han YOLO | |

One Ford is a dangerous human
fugitive who was framed by the
government, and the other is an
indestructible synthetic killing
machine from the future – but no one
knows for sure which one is which.
As opponents waste time
trying to spot the difference,
they are wiped out.

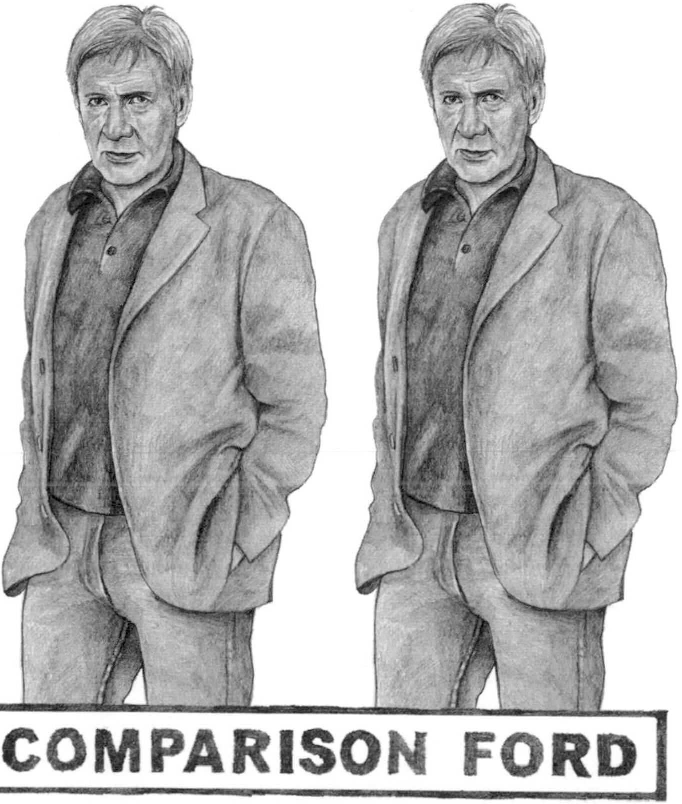

COMPARISON FORD

WORK RATE
Disrupts picnics

85

INTELLIGENCE
Crazy right now

32

STRENGTH
Finds a way to put a sting on it

71

SPEED
Runs the world

81

AGGRESSION
Sasha fierce

92

Beeyoncé's status as the Queen of Pop is actually due to her habit of sniffing out soft drinks – especially lemonade – and other sugary foods. She hovers above them producing musical vibrations, which make listeners feel that anything is possible if they believe in themselves. She then swoops down and pulls off their heads with her thighs.

BEEYONCÉ

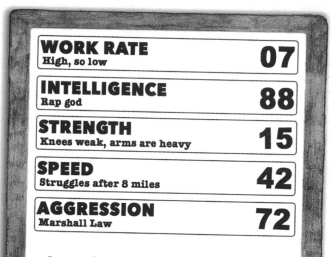

WORK RATE
High, so low
07

INTELLIGENCE
Rap god
88

STRENGTH
Knees weak, arms are heavy
15

SPEED
Struggles after 8 miles
42

AGGRESSION
Marshall Law
72

A terrifying blend of man and confectionery, this chilling creature incapacitates his victims with his fast-moving rhymes before inducing anaphylactic shock with his nutty core.

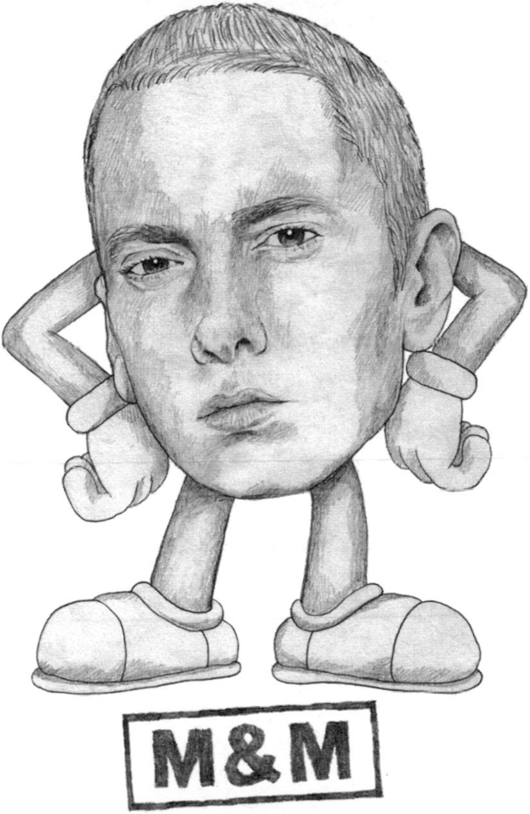

M&M

WORK RATE	**11**
Turn it up to Ocean's Eleven	

INTELLIGENCE	**67**
Learns after reading	

STRENGTH	**63**
Wired differently	

SPEED	**29**
Snail Caesar	

AGGRESSION	**91**
Intolerable cruelty	

When he was struck by lightning, holding a low-quality espresso, George became addicted to terrible coffee. Now he has been forced to advertise it in exchange for a constant supply. His jittery bad-breathed attacks can only be avoided by reminding him what a terrible Batman he was.

GEORGE LOONEY

WORK RATE	39
Tinker, tailor, strolling by	

INTELLIGENCE	94
It's all elementary	

STRENGTH	57
Intimidation game	

SPEED	67
Legs Benedict	

AGGRESSION	70
Wrath of Khan	

Cumberpatch heads up a ruthless and secretive international crime syndicate, known as the Cruel Cumbers. Specializing in prostitution, people trafficking, and competitively priced spa and sauna packages, Cumberpatch has the world cowering at his feet.

BENEDICT CUMBERPATCH